Top 50
Pandas
Interview
Questions &
Answers

Knowledge Powerhouse

DEDICATION

To our readers!

CONTENTS

ACKNOWLEDGMENTS

We thank our readers who constantly send feedback and reviews to motivate us in creating these useful books with the latest information!

INTRODUCTION

Machine Learning is one of the fastest growing technology trends. There is a growing demand for Pandas and Python in technology companies.

This book contains technical interview questions that an interviewer asks on Pandas subject. Each question is accompanied with an answer so that you can prepare for job interview in short time.

We have compiled this list after attending dozens of technical interviews in top-notch companies like- Uber, IBM, Oracle etc.

Often, these questions and concepts are used in our daily work. But these are most helpful when an Interviewer is trying to test your deep knowledge of Pandas.

Once you go through them in the first pass, mark the questions that you could not answer. Then, in second pass go through only the difficult questions. After going through this book 2-3 times, you will be well prepared to face a technical interview in Pandas area.

Pandas Interview Questions

1. What is Pandas?

Pandas is a Python library that provides data structures and tools to analyze data in Python language.

It is an open source library and it has a very rich set of library functions for data analysis.

It is used in finance, statistics, and economics etc. fields.

2. What are the key features of Pandas library?

Some of the key features of Pandas are as follows:

- **DataFrame**: Pandas provides DataFrame object to customize the handling of data.
- **Data alignment**: Pandas provides functions to populate missing data with default values and align the features of data.
- **Memory efficient**: Pandas can help in loading the data in memory that provides high performance data analysis.
- **Reshaping**: We can use pivot functions to reshape the data in Pandas.
- **Column addition**: We can easily add or delete columns in data by using Pandas.

- **Merging and Join**: Pandas provides functions to operations like merge and join similar to database queries in python.
- **Time series**: Pandas also gives Time series feature to view data. We can analyze data over a frequency of periods like months, weeks etc by using Time series.

3. What are the different types of data structures in pandas?

Some of the main types of data structures in pandas are as follows:

- **Series**: It is a one dimensional data structure in Pandas.
- **DataFrame**: It is a two-dimension data structure in Pandas.
- **Panel**: It is used for storing 3-dimensional data in Pandas.

4. What is a Series in Pandas?

Series is a like an array in Pandas. It is used to store one-dimensional data.

We can store homogenous data in a series in Pandas. The values in series are mutable.

The axis labels in a series are called index.

E.g. s = pd.Series(testData, index=index)
This can be used to create a series from testData. We can use a Python dict, ndarray or a scalar value to create the testData.

Following code snippet uses Numpy library to create a series of 5 random numbers.

s = pd.Series(np.random.randn(5))

5. How can we create copy of series in Pandas?

We can call copy() function on a series in Pandas to create a copy.

E.g. s2 = s1.copy() will create copy of series s1 in a new series s2.

We can create shallow as well as deep copy of a series in Pandas.

Shallow copy shares data and index with the original series.

Deep copy has its own copy of data and index.

s2_deep = s1.copy(deep=True)

6. How will you create a series

from dict in Python?

We can pass dict as an input parameter to Series() function in Pandas.

E.g.
import pandas as pd
import numpy as np
data = {'a':0,'b':1}
s = pd.Series(data)

In this example we have created a series from dict data.

7. What are operations on Series in pandas?

We can use operations to access data in a Series.

In following example we are retrieving the element at first position in a Series.
import pandas as pd
s = pd.Series([1,2,3],index = ['a','b','c'])

#retrieve the second element
print s[1]

8. What is a DataFrame in pandas?

A DataFrame in pandas is a two-dimension data structure. It is like a table in sql or a spreadsheet. It has rows and columns.

It is a mutable data structure. We can change the values of data inside a DataFrame.

DataFrame is a heterogeneous data structure.

It has labeled axes of rows and columns.

It can be considered as a dict like structure for Series objects.

E.g. In following example we are creating a DataFrame.

```
>>> inputdata = {'column1': [10, 20], 'column2': [30, 40]}
>>> dframe = pd.DataFrame(data=inputdata)
>>> dframe
   col1  col2
0   10    30
1   20    40
```

9. What are the different ways in which a DataFrame can be created in Pandas?

We can create a DataFrame object by one of the following ways:

dict:
```
inputdata = [['A',10],['B',20],['C',30]]
dframe= pd.DataFrame(inputdata,
columns=['Name','ID'], dtype=float)
```

List:
```
inputdata = [10,20,30]
dframe= pd.DataFrame(inputdata)
```

Series

ndarray of numpy
Copy of another DataFrame

10. How will you create an empty DataFrame in pandas?

We can create an empty DataFrame in pandas as follows:

```
import pandas as pd
df = pd.DataFrame()
```

After creating the empty DataFrame, we can add columns to DataFrame.

11. How will you add a column to a pandas DataFrame?

We can add a column to a pandas DataFrame as follows:

Create an empty DataFrame
```
import pandas as pd
df = pd.DataFrame()
```

Add a column
```
df['ID'] = pd.Series([10,20,30], index=['a','b','c'])
df
```

Output:
    ID

```
a    10
b    20
c    30
```

12. How will you add a scalar column with same value for all rows to a pandas DataFrame?

We can add a scalar with same value to a DataFrame as follows:

Create an empty DataFrame:
import pandas as pd
df = pd.DataFrame()

Add a column
df['ID'] = pd.Series([10,20,30], index=['a','b','c'])

Add a scalar column
df['AGE'] = 20
df

Output:

	ID	AGE
a	10	20
b	20	20
c	30	20

The above code adds AGE column to each row with scalar value 20.

13. How will you retrieve a single column from pandas DataFrame?

If we take previous example and create DataFrame, we can retrieve the ID column as follows:

Create an empty DataFrame
import pandas as pd
df = pd.DataFrame()

Add a column
df['ID'] = pd.Series([10,20,30], index=['a','b','c'])

Add a scalar column
df['AGE'] = 20

Retrieve ID column
df['ID']

Output:
```
      ID
a     10
b     20
c     30
```

14. How will you add the value of two columns in a pandas DataFrame to create another column?

We can create a new column by adding the values of two columns in a pandas DataFrame as follows:

Create an empty DataFrame
import pandas as pd
df = pd.DataFrame()

Add a column
df['ID'] = pd.Series([10,20,30], index=['a','b','c'])

Add a scalar column
df['AGE'] = 20

Create another column
df['SUM'] = df['AGE] + df['ID']
df['SUM']

Output:

```
    SUM
a   30
b   40
c   50
```

15. How will you delete a column in a pandas DataFrame?

We can delete a column in a pandas DataFrame following ways:

- **Delete a column**
  del df['SUM']

- **Pop a column**
  df.pop('SUM')

16. How can we select a column in pandas DataFrame?

We can select a column in pandas DataFrame as follows:

In following example we are selecting the column ID from data frame.

```
import pandas as pd
df = pd.DataFrame()
df['ID'] = pd.Series([10,20,30], index=['a','b','c'])
df['AGE'] = 20
df['ID']
```

Output:
```
a    10
b    20
c    30
Name: ID, dtype: int64
```

17. How can we retrieve a row in pandas DataFrame?

We can use following ways to retrieve a row in pandas DataFrame:

By Label:

In following example we are retrieving the row 'a' by label:

```
import pandas as pd
df = pd.DataFrame()
df['ID'] = pd.Series([10,20,30], index=['a','b','c'])
df['AGE'] = 20
df.loc['a']
```

Output:

```
ID    10
AGE    20
Name: a dtype: int64
```

By Integer location:

In following example we are retrieving the second row by integer location:

```
import pandas as pd
df = pd.DataFrame()
df['ID'] = pd.Series([10,20,30], index=['a','b','c'])
df['AGE'] = 20
df.iloc[2]
```

Output:

```
ID    20
AGE    20
Name: b dtype: int64
```

18. How will you slice rows in a pandas DataFrame?

In a pandas DataFrame we can select a specific range of rows. It is called slicing.

We can do slicing as follows:
```
import pandas as pd
df = pd.DataFrame()
df['ID'] = pd.Series([10,20,30], index=['a','b','c'])
df['AGE'] = 20
```

First row:
In this example we are getting first row.
```
df[:1]
```
	ID	AGE
a	10	20

Last row:
In this example we are getting last row. The negative number means row starting from the end.
```
df[-1:]
```
	ID	AGE
c	30	20

Row from 1 to 2:
In this example we are getting row 1 to 2. In this case first element is excluded. So we are getting only second row.
```
df[1:2]
```
	ID	AGE
b	20	20

19. How will you append new rows to a pandas DataFrame?

We can use append function to add new rows to a pandas DataFrame.

```
import numpy as np
import pandas as pd
df = pd.DataFrame()
df['ID'] = pd.Series([10,20,30], index=['a','b','c'])
df['AGE'] = 20
```

Creating new data frame called newdf
```
newdf = pd.DataFrame([[40, 20]], columns =
['ID','AGE'],index=['d'])
```

Append the new data frame to existing df.
```
df = df.append(newdf)
df
```

Output:

	ID	AGE
a	10	20
b	20	20
c	30	20
d	40	20

20. How will you delete rows from a pandas DataFrame?

We can use drop function to drop rows from a pandas DataFrame. We have to pass the label of the row to be dropped.

```
import numpy as np
import pandas as pd
df = pd.DataFrame()
df['ID'] = pd.Series([10,20,30], index=['a','b','c'])
df['AGE'] = 20
```

Dropping the row with label 'a'
```
df = df.drop('a')
df
```

Output:

	ID	AGE
b	20	20
c	30	20

21. How will you get the number of rows and columns of a DataFrame in pandas?

We can use the shape attribute to get the count of rows and columns of a DataFrame in pandas.

```
import numpy as np
import pandas as pd
df = pd.DataFrame()
df['ID'] = pd.Series([10,20,30], index=['a','b','c'])
df['AGE'] = 20
```

df.shape

Output:

(3,2)
There are 3 rows with two columns in this DataFrame.

22. How will you get the top 2 rows from a DataFrame in pandas?

We can use head() function to get the top 2 rows from a DataFrame in pandas.

```
import numpy as np
import pandas as pd
df = pd.DataFrame()
df['ID'] = pd.Series([10,20,30], index=['a','b','c'])
df['AGE'] = 20
```

df.head(2)

Output:

	ID	AGE
a	10	20
b	20	20

23. How will you get the last 2 rows from a DataFrame in pandas?

We can use tail() function to get the last 2 rows from a DataFrame in pandas.

```
import numpy as np
import pandas as pd
df = pd.DataFrame()
df['ID'] = pd.Series([10,20,30], index=['a','b','c'])
df['AGE'] = 20
```

df.tail(2)

Output:

	ID	AGE
b	20	20
c	30	20

24. How will you get the number of elements in a DataFrame in pandas?

We can use size attribute to get the number of elements in a DataFrame in pandas.

```
import numpy as np
import pandas as pd
df = pd.DataFrame()
df['ID'] = pd.Series([10,20,30], index=['a','b','c'])
df['AGE'] = 20
```

df.size

Output:

6

25. How will you get the names of columns of a DataFrame in pandas?

In pandas, column as well as rows are considered as axes of DataFrame. We can read the DataFrame by column or by row.

Therefore, row as well as column is a kind of axis. To get the axes of a DataFrame we call the axes attribute.

In following example we are getting the names of columns as well as labels of each row.

```
import numpy as np
import pandas as pd
df = pd.DataFrame()
df['ID'] = pd.Series([10,20,30], index=['a','b','c'])
df['AGE'] = 20
```

df.axes

Output:

[Index(['a', 'b', 'c'], dtype='object'), Index(['ID', 'AGE'], dtype='object')]

26. How will you convert a DataFrame to an array in pandas?

We can use values attribute to convert the DataFrame into an array in pandas. It actually does not do any conversion. It just provides us the values in an array format.

```
import numpy as np
import pandas as pd
df = pd.DataFrame()
df['ID'] = pd.Series([10,20,30], index=['a','b','c'])
df['AGE'] = 20
```

df.values

Output:

```
array([[10, 20],
       [20, 20],
       [30, 20]])
```

27. How can you check if a DataFrame is empty in pandas?

We can use empty attribute the check is a DataFrame is empty. It returns True, if the DataFrame is empty.

In following example we get False, because data frame is not empty.
```
import numpy as np
import pandas as pd
df = pd.DataFrame()
df['ID'] = pd.Series([10,20,30], index=['a','b','c'])
df['AGE'] = 20
```

df.empty

Output:

False

28. How can you get the sum of values of a column in pandas DataFrame?

We can use sum() function to get the sum of the values of a column in pandas DataFrame.

In following example we are getting the sum of column ID and column AGE.

```
import numpy as np
import pandas as pd
df = pd.DataFrame()
df['ID'] = pd.Series([10,20,30], index=['a','b','c'])
df['AGE'] = 20
```

df.sum()

Output:

```
ID    60
AGE   60
dtype: int64
```

29. How will you get the average of values of a column in pandas DataFrame?

We can use mean() function to get the average of the

values of a column in pandas DataFrame.

In following example we are getting the mean of column ID and column AGE.

```
import numpy as np
import pandas as pd
df = pd.DataFrame()
df['ID'] = pd.Series([10,20,30], index=['a','b','c'])
df['AGE'] = 20
```

df.mean()

Output:

```
ID     20.0
AGE    20.0
dtype: float64
```

30. How can we get the statistical summary of data in a pandas DataFrame?

We can use describe() function to get the summary of data in a pandas DataFrame.
In summary, we get the sum, count, mean etc. details of data.

In following example we are getting the summary of data.

```
import numpy as np
import pandas as pd
df = pd.DataFrame()
df['ID'] = pd.Series([10,20,30], index=['a','b','c'])
df['AGE'] = 20
```

df.describe()

Output:

	ID	AGE
count	3.0	3.0
mean	20.0	20.0
std	10.0	0.0
min	10.0	20.0
25%	15.0	20.0
50%	20.0	20.0
75%	25.0	20.0
max	30.0	20.0

31. How will you apply a function to every data element in a DataFrame?

We can use pipe() function to apply a function to every data element in a pandas DataFrame. We have to first define the function. Then we can pass it to pipe() function.

In following example we are adding 5 to every element of data frame.

```
import numpy as np
import pandas as pd
df = pd.DataFrame()
df['ID'] = pd.Series([10,20,30], index=['a','b','c'])
df['AGE'] = 20

def adder(ele1,ele2):
    return ele1+ele2
```

df.pipe(adder,5)

Output:

	ID	AGE
a	15	25
b	25	25
c	35	25

32. How will you apply a function to a row of pandas DataFrame?

We can use apply() function to apply a lambda function to a row in a pandas DataFrame. We have to first create a lambda function and pass it to a specific row by using slicing method.

In following example we are using :1 to get the first row of DataFrame. Then we multiply the values of this row with 5 by using a lambda function. Then we use apply function to apply this lambda function to each value of this row.

```
import numpy as np
import pandas as pd

df = pd.DataFrame()
df['ID'] = pd.Series([10,20,30], index=[1,2,3])
df['AGE'] = 20

df[:1] = df[:1].apply(lambda x:x*5,axis=1)
df
```

Output:

	ID	AGE
1	50	100
2	20	20
3	30	20

33. How will you apply a function to a column of pandas DataFrame?

We can use apply() function to apply a lambda function to a column in a pandas DataFrame. We have to first create a lambda function and pass it to a specific column.

In following example we are using ['ID'] to get the first column of DataFrame. Then we multiply the values of this column with 5 by using a lambda function. Then we use apply() function to apply this lambda function to each value of ID column.

```
import numpy as np
import pandas as pd

df = pd.DataFrame()
df['ID'] = pd.Series([10,20,30], index=[1,2,3])
df['AGE'] = 20

df['ID'] = df['ID'].apply(lambda x:x*5)
df
```

Output:

```
ID    AGE
1    50    20
2    100   20
3    150   20
```

34. What is reindexing in pandas?

We use reindexing in pandas to change the labels and column names of a DataFrame. We can also create a new DataFrame with the subset of data from original DataFrame by reindexing.

We use reindex() function on a data frame for this purpose.

We can use reindexing to change the ordering of existing data with the new set of labels. We can also insert NA or NaN values while doing reindexing.

In following example we are reindexing the original data frame, by adding a NaN column to data and selecting only first two rows.

```
import numpy as np
import pandas as pd

df = pd.DataFrame()
df['ID'] = pd.Series([10,20,30], index=[1,2,3])
df['AGE'] = 20

df_reindex = df.reindex(index=[1,2],
columns=['ID','AGE','STATUS'])

df_reindex
```

Output:

```
   ID    AGE   STATUS
1  10.0  20.0  NaN
2  20.0  20.0  NaN
```

35. How will you rename a column in pandas DataFrame?

We can use rename() function to rename a column in a pandas DataFrame.

In following example we are renaming column AGE as YEARS. We use the parameter inplace=True to change the existing data frame.

```
import numpy as np
import pandas as pd

df = pd.DataFrame()
df['ID'] = pd.Series([10,20,30], index=[1,2,3])
df['AGE'] = 20

df.rename(columns={'AGE':'YEARS'}, inplace=True)
df
```

Output:

```
   ID   YEARS
1  10   20
2  20   20
3  30   20
```

36. How will you iterate through all the items in a pandas DataFrame?

We can use the functions like iteritems(), iterrows(), itertyples() to iterate through all the items in a pandas DataFrame.

The usage of these functions is as follows:
iteritems(): It is used to iterate over each item in a DataFrame. It gives key,value pair as output. It gives each column's data.

```
import numpy as np
import pandas as pd

df = pd.DataFrame()
df['ID'] = pd.Series([10,20,30], index=[1,2,3])
df['AGE'] = 20

for col in df.iteritems():
    print(col)

('ID', 1    10
2    20
3    30
Name: ID, dtype: int64)
('AGE', 1    20
2    20
```

```
3    20
Name: AGE, dtype: int64)
```

iterrows(): It is used to iterate over each row. It gives index,series pair as output.

```
import numpy as np
import pandas as pd

df = pd.DataFrame()
df['ID'] = pd.Series([10,20,30], index=[1,2,3])
df['AGE'] = 20

for row in df.iterrows():
    print(row)
```

```
(1, ID    10
AGE    20
Name: 1, dtype: int64)
(2, ID    20
AGE    20
Name: 2, dtype: int64)
(3, ID    30
AGE    20
Name: 3, dtype: int64)
```

itertuples(): It is used to iterate over rows as named tuple.

```
import numpy as np
import pandas as pd

df = pd.DataFrame()
df['ID'] = pd.Series([10,20,30], index=[1,2,3])
df['AGE'] = 20
```

```
for row in df.itertuples():
```

    print(row)

Output:

Pandas(Index=1, ID=10, AGE=20)
Pandas(Index=2, ID=20, AGE=20)
Pandas(Index=3, ID=30, AGE=20)

37. Can we modify the data in a DataFrame while iterating over it?

Yes, we can modify the data in a DataFrame during iteration. But the changes are not reflected in the original DataFrame.

The purpose of iterating is to read the values. It should not be used for updates.

38. What are the different sorting options available in pandas DataFrame?

We can use following sorting options in a pandas DataFrame.
   • **Sort by Label:** Pandas function sort_index() is used for sorting by label.
We have to specify the axis argument and sort by (ascending or descending) option to sort the data.

Following code sorts the data in descending order of label.
import numpy as np
import pandas as pd

```
df = pd.DataFrame()
df['ID'] = pd.Series([10,20,30], index=[1,2,3])
df['AGE'] = 20

sorted_df=df.sort_index(ascending=False)
sorted_df
```

Output:

	ID	AGE
3	30	20
2	20	20
1	10	20

We can pass axis = 0 to sort by rows. We can pass axis = 1 to sort by columns.

- **Sort by Actual value:** We can also sort the data in a DataFrame by specifying the column name. We use sort_values() function for this purpose.

In this example we are sorting by column ID in descending order.

```
import numpy as np
import pandas as pd

df = pd.DataFrame()
df['ID'] = pd.Series([10,20,30], index=[1,2,3])
df['AGE'] = 20

sorted_df=df.sort_values(by='ID',ascending=False)
sorted_df
```

Output:

```
     ID   AGE
3    30   20
2    20   20
1    10   20
```

39. Can we specify a sorting algorithm to pandas DataFrame during sorting?

Yes, we can specify the sorting algorithm like heap sort, merge sort etc to pandas DataFrame during sorting operation.

We pass kind parameter and the name of algorithm to sort_values() function.

In following example we are using quick sort algorithm to sort the data.

```
import numpy as np
import pandas as pd

df = pd.DataFrame()
df['ID'] = pd.Series([10,20,30], index=[1,2,3])
df['AGE'] = 20

sorted_df=df.sort_values(by='ID',kind='quicksort')
sorted_df
```

Output:

```
   ID    AGE
```

```
1    10    20
2    20    20
3    30    20
```

40. What are the different string manipulation functions provides by pandas?

Pandas provides useful string manipulation functions to modify the text data in a Series. Some of these functions are as follows:

upper(): This function changes the case of text to uppercase. It works on each element of the series.

Following code changes the case to uppercase.

```
import numpy as np
import pandas as pd

s = pd.Series(['a', 'b', 'c'])
s.str.upper()
```

```
0    A
1    B
2    C
dtype: object
```

lower(): This function changes the case of text to lowercase. It works on each element of the series.

Following code changes the case to lowercase.

```
import numpy as np
import pandas as pd
```

```
s = pd.Series(['A', 'B', 'C'])
s.str.lower()
```

Output:

```
0    a
1    b
2    c
dtype: object
```

len() : This function gives the length of the string.

```
import numpy as np
import pandas as pd

s = pd.Series(['A', 'BB', 'CCC'])
s.str.len()
```

```
0    1
1    2
2    3
dtype: int64
```

strip(): This function removes white spaces from beginning and end of the text.

startswith(): This function returns true if an element starts with a specific pattern.

endswith(): This function returns true if an element ends with a specific pattern.

replace(a,b): This function replaces the value a with the value b in an element.

41. What are the different options in pandas to index a DataFrame?

We can use following options in pandas to index a DataFrame:

- **.loc :** This is label based indexing technique. We can get rows or columns with a particular label from the index.

In following example we are getting ID column for every row in data frame. For every row we are passing : as parameter and for ID column we are passing ID as option to loc() function.

```
import numpy as np
import pandas as pd

df = pd.DataFrame()
df['ID'] = pd.Series([10,20,30], index=[1,2,3])
df['AGE'] = 20

df.loc[:,'ID']
```

Output:

```
1    10
2    20
3    30
Name: ID, dtype: int64
```

- **.iloc:** This is integer based indexing option. We can get rows or columns at a specific position in the index.

In following example we are getting row 1 to 3 and 2nd column from data frame. For row 1 to 3 we are passing 1:3 and for column AGE we are passing 2 as parameters to iloc() function.

```
import numpy as np
import pandas as pd

df = pd.DataFrame()
df['ID'] = pd.Series([10,20,30], index=[1,2,3])
df['AGE'] = 20

df.iloc[1:3,1]
```

Output:

```
2    20
3    20
Name: AGE, dtype: int64
```

42. How can we get the percent of change between elements of a data frame?

We can use pct_change() function to calculate the percent of change between elements of a data frame.

The default option in pct_change is to work on column. In case we want to get percent change between the values of same row we can pass axis=1 as parameter.

In case there is no change in the value it gives 0 as the

result. In case, there is no previous element, it gives NaN as result.

Eg.
```
import numpy as np
import pandas as pd

df = pd.DataFrame()
df['ID'] = pd.Series([10,20,30], index=[1,2,3])
df['AGE'] = 20
df.pct_change()
```

Original df:
```
   ID   AGE
1  10   20
2  20   20
3  30   20
```

Output:

Result of pct_change:

```
ID    AGE
1  NaN   NaN
2  1.0   0.0
3  0.5   0.0
```

43. How can we calculate the covariance between elements of a DataFrame?

We can use cov function to calculate covariance between the elements of a DataFrame. The output of this function is the covariance result of a series. In a DataFrame, a column can be considered as a series.

Eg. In following example we are calculating covariance of ID and AGE columns.

```
import numpy as np
import pandas as pd

df = pd.DataFrame()
df['ID'] = pd.Series([10,20,30], index=[1,2,3])
df['AGE'] = 20
df.cov()
```

Output:

	ID	AGE
ID	100.0	0.0
AGE	0.0	0.0

44. How will you calculate the correlation between the values of pandas DataFrame?

We can use corr() function to calculate the correlation between the values of a pandas DataFrame. Correlation is the linear relation between two series.

In following example, ID is 10, 20 ,30 and AGE is 1, 2, and 3. Therefore data is linearly correlated.

```
import numpy as np
import pandas as pd
```

```
df = pd.DataFrame()
df['ID'] = pd.Series([10,20,30], index=[1,2,3])
df['AGE'] = pd.Series([1,2,3], index=[1,2,3])
df['ID'].corr(df['AGE'])
```

Output:

1.0

45. How will you rank the data in a pandas DataFrame?

We can use rank() function to find the rank of a data element in pandas DataFrame. rank() function finds the rank in increasing order. In case of tie, it gives mean rank as output.

In following example we are getting the rank 1, 2, 3 for ID 10, 20, 30. Whereas we are getting same mean rank 2 for AGE 20, 20 , 20.

```
import numpy as np
import pandas as pd

df = pd.DataFrame()
df['ID'] = pd.Series([10,20,30], index=[1,2,3])
df['AGE'] = 20
df.rank()
```

Output:

ID   AGE

```
1   1.0   2.0
2   2.0   2.0
3   3.0   2.0
```

46. What is the use of rolling() function in pandas DataFrame?

We can use rolling() function to calculate the statistical values of a specified number of elements of a DataFrame. In case we have to calculate mean, median, sum etc of 3 neighboring elements, then we can use window=3 parameter of rolling function.

In following example we are calculating mean() of 3 consecutive elements of a DataFrame.

```
import numpy as np
import pandas as pd

df = pd.DataFrame()
df['ID'] = pd.Series([10,20,30,40,50], index=[1,2,3,4,5])
df['AGE'] = 20
df.rolling(window=3).mean()
```

Output:

```
    ID     AGE
1   NaN    NaN
2   NaN    NaN
3   20.0   20.0
4   30.0   20.0
5   40.0   20.0
```

47. How will you get the pandas version installed on your system or notebook?

We can use pd.__version__ to get the version of pandas installed on the system.

E.g. pd.__version__
'0.19.2'

48. How will you group by data in a pandas DataFrame?

We can use groupby function to group the data of a column in a pandas DataFrame. Once the data is grouped, we can calculate the mean, sum, count etc of that column.

In following example we are calculating the mean of data after grouping by ID column.

```
import numpy as np
import pandas as pd


df = pd.DataFrame()
df['ID'] = pd.Series([10,20,30,40,50], index=[1,2,3,4,5])
df['AGE'] = 20


df.groupby(['ID']).mean()
```

Output:

```
    AGE
ID
10    20
20    20
30    20
40    20
50    20
```

In following example we are grouping by AGE and getting the count. Since all the elements have age 20, count is 5.

```
import numpy as np
import pandas as pd


df = pd.DataFrame()
df['ID'] = pd.Series([10,20,30,40,50], index=[1,2,3,4,5])
df['AGE'] = 20

df.groupby(['AGE']).count()
```

```
    ID
AGE
20    5
```

Group by in pandas works similar to group by in SQL.

49. How will you deal with missing data in pandas DataFrame?

Often we find missing data values in a pandas DataFrame.

This can be due to error in data collection or unwillingness of users to fill data completely in a survey.

We can use isnull(), notnull(), fillna() and dropna() functions to deal with missing data in a pandas DataFrame.

In following example we have NaN value for SCORE in a column.

```
import numpy as np
import pandas as pd


df = pd.DataFrame()
df['ID'] = pd.Series([10,20,30], index=[1,2,3])
df['AGE'] = 20
df['SCORE'] = pd.Series([100,200], index=[1,2])

df
```

Output:

ID	AGE	SCORE
1	10	20	100.0
2	20	20	200.0
3	30	20	NaN

We can use following code to get the values of SCORE that are null

```
df['SCORE'].isnull()
```

```
1    False
2    False
3    True
```

Name: SCORE, dtype: bool

We can use fillna() function to fill NaN values with a number. In following example we are filling 0 in place of null score.

```
import numpy as np
import pandas as pd


df = pd.DataFrame()
df['ID'] = pd.Series([10,20,30], index=[1,2,3])
df['AGE'] = 20
df['SCORE'] = pd.Series([100,200], index=[1,2])
df = df.fillna(0)
df['SCORE'].isnull()
```

```
1    False
2    False
3    False
Name: SCORE, dtype: bool
```

We can also use dropna() function to drop the records with Nan values.

In following example we are dropping the Nan values in data frame.

```
import numpy as np
import pandas as pd


df = pd.DataFrame()
df['ID'] = pd.Series([10,20,30], index=[1,2,3])
df['AGE'] = 20
df['SCORE'] = pd.Series([100,200], index=[1,2])
```

```
df = df.dropna()
df['SCORE'].isnull()
```

```
1    False
2    False
Name: SCORE, dtype: bool
```

50. How will you filter data in a pandas DataFrame?

We can use filter() function to get filtered data based on a column name in a pandas DataFrame.

In following example we are filtering data frame with AGE column.

```
import numpy as np
import pandas as pd
```

```
df = pd.DataFrame()
df['ID'] = pd.Series([10,20,30], index=[1,2,3])
df['AGE'] = 20
df.filter(items=['AGE'])
```

Output:

```
   AGE
1   20
2   20
3   20
```

In following example we are filtering by the columns that

contain A in the name.

```
import numpy as np
import pandas as pd


df = pd.DataFrame()
df['AD'] = pd.Series([10,20,30], index=[1,2,3])
df['AGE'] = 20
df['SCORE'] = 50
df.filter(regex='A', axis=1)
```

Output:

	AD	AGE
1	10	20
2	20	20
3	30	20

BONUS QUESTIONS

51. How will you perform a SQL join like operation on pandas DataFrame?

We can use merge function to perform SQL join like operation on a pandas DataFrame.

We can perform left, right, inner join etc in SQL style by using merge function.

In following example, we are merging two data frames based on ID column.

```
import numpy as np
import pandas as pd


leftdf = pd.DataFrame()
leftdf['ID'] = pd.Series([10,20,30], index=[1,2,3])
leftdf['AGE'] = 20

rightdf = pd.DataFrame()
rightdf['ID'] = pd.Series([10,20,30], index=[1,2,3])
rightdf['SCORE'] = 50

pd.merge(leftdf,rightdf,on='ID')
```

```
ID   AGE   SCORE
0    10    20    50
1    20    20    50
2    30    20    50
```

In following example right data frame has only two elements. Due to this the result of join has only two rows.

```
import numpy as np
import pandas as pd


leftdf = pd.DataFrame()
leftdf['ID'] = pd.Series([10,20,30], index=[1,2,3])
leftdf['AGE'] = 20

rightdf = pd.DataFrame()
rightdf['ID'] = pd.Series([10,20], index=[1,2])
rightdf['SCORE'] = 50

pd.merge(leftdf,rightdf,on='ID')
```

	ID	AGE	SCORE
0	10	20	50
1	20	20	50

In case we want all the rows from left data frame, we can use how parameter with left option.

```
import numpy as np
import pandas as pd


leftdf = pd.DataFrame()
leftdf['ID'] = pd.Series([10,20,30], index=[1,2,3])
leftdf['AGE'] = 20

rightdf = pd.DataFrame()
rightdf['ID'] = pd.Series([10,20], index=[1,2])
rightdf['SCORE'] = 50

pd.merge(leftdf,rightdf,on='ID', how='left')
```

Output:

```
ID   AGE   SCORE
0    10    20    50.0
1    20    20    50.0
2    30    20    NaN
```

52. How will you concatenate two data frames in pandas?

We can use concat function to concatenate two data frames in pandas.

In following example we are concatenating two data frames to create data frame with combined elements from both the data frames.

```
import numpy as np
import pandas as pd


leftdf = pd.DataFrame()
leftdf['ID'] = pd.Series([10,20,30], index=[1,2,3])
leftdf['AGE'] = 20

rightdf = pd.DataFrame()
rightdf['ID'] = pd.Series([40,50], index=[4,5])
rightdf['AGE'] = 50

pd.concat([leftdf,rightdf])
```

Output:

```
   ID   AGE
```

```
1   10   20
2   20   20
3   30   20
4   40   50
5   50   50
```

We can even associate keys with the concatenated data in above example.

pd.concat([leftdf,rightdf],keys=['A','B'])

Output:

```
        AGE   ID
A   1   20.0   10
    2   20.0   20
    3   20.0   30
B   4   NaN    40
    5   NaN    50
```

53. What is a TimeSeries in pandas?

Pandas provides a useful feature of working with time-based data like dates, time of day etc.

We can use pd.datetime.now() to get the current time.
pd.datetime.now()
datetime.datetime(2018, 9, 4, 12, 22, 40, 318093)

54. How will you create a time stamp in pandas?

We can use Timestamp() function to create a time stamp for a specific time in pandas.

This function has inbuilt mechanism to check for incorrect data and invalid dates passed to it.

Following code creates a timestamp object with date 30 November 2020.

```
pd.Timestamp('2020-11-30')
```

55. How will you convert date time like data into date time objects in pandas?

We can use to_datetime() function to convert date time like data in various formats to date time objects in pandas.

E.g.

```
import numpy as np
import pandas as pd


pd.to_datetime(pd.Series(['Sep    30, 2019','2020-01-10','2020-August-10']))
```

Output:

```
0   2019-09-30
1   2020-01-10
2   2020-08-10
dtype: datetime64[ns]
```

56. What is NaT in pandas?

In pandas, NaT refers to Not a time. It is similar to NaN, not a number.

Any invalid date format data is considered as NaT in pandas.

57. What is categorical data in pandas?

In real life, we come across various categories of data like-country, city, gender etc. The data in these categories is often repetitive data. It is called categorical data in pandas.

The categorical data can be expressed as a finite list of values.

We can create a categorical data series as follows in pandas:

```
import pandas as pd
grade = pd.Series(["A","B","C"], dtype="category")
grade
```

```
0   A
1   B
2   C
dtype: category
Categories (3, object): [A, B, C]
```

We can also use Categorical constructor to create a category object in pandas.

```
import pandas as pd
grade = pd.Categorical(['A', 'B', 'C'])
grade
```

```
[A, B, C]
Categories (3, object): [A, B, C]
```

58. How will you create a bar chart from a column in pandas data frame?

We can use plot and bar function() to create a bar chart.

In following example we are creating a bar chart of ID column.

```
import numpy as np
import pandas as pd

df = pd.DataFrame()
df['ID'] = pd.Series([10,20,30], index=[1,2,3])
df['AGE'] = 20
ax = df.plot.bar(y='ID', rot=0)
```

59. How will you create a bar chart by aggregating values

from two columns in pandas data frame?

We can use plot and bar function() to create a bar chart. If we use parameter stacked, it aggregates the values from two columns.

In following example we are creating a bar chart of ID and AGE column stacked.

```
import numpy as np
import pandas as pd

df = pd.DataFrame()
df['ID'] = pd.Series([10,20,30], index=[1,2,3])
df['AGE'] = 20
ax = df.plot.bar(stacked=True)
```

60. How will you create a horizontal bar chart from a column in pandas data frame?

We can use plot and barh function() to create a horizontal bar chart.

In following example we are creating a horizontal bar chart of ID column.

```
import numpy as np
import pandas as pd

df = pd.DataFrame()
df['ID'] = pd.Series([10,20,30], index=[1,2,3])
```

```
df['AGE'] = 20
ax = df.plot.barh(y='ID', rot=0)
```

61. How will you create a histogram of a column in pandas data frame?

We can use plot and hist function() to create a histogram chart.

In following example we are creating a histogram chart of ID column.

```
import numpy as np
import pandas as pd

df = pd.DataFrame()
df['ID'] = pd.Series([10,20,30], index=[1,2,3])
df['AGE'] = 20
df.plot.hist()
```

62. How will you create a box plot in pandas data frame?

We can use plot and box() functions to create box plot of a pandas data frame.

In following example we are creating a box plot of a pandas data frame.

```
import numpy as np
```

```
import pandas as pd

df = pd.DataFrame()
df['ID'] = pd.Series([10,20,30], index=[1,2,3])
df['AGE'] = 20
df.plot.box()
```

63. How will you create an area plot in pandas data frame?

We can use plot and area() functions to create area plot of a pandas data frame.

In following example we are creating a area plot of a pandas data frame.

```
import numpy as np
import pandas as pd

df = pd.DataFrame()
df['ID'] = pd.Series([10,20,30], index=[1,2,3])
df['AGE'] = 20
df.plot.area()
```

64. How will you create a scatter plot in pandas data frame?

We can use plot and scatter() functions to create scatter plot of a pandas data frame.

In following example we are creating a scatter plot of a pandas data frame.

```
import numpy as np
import pandas as pd

df = pd.DataFrame()
df['ID'] = pd.Series([10,20,30], index=[1,2,3])
df['AGE'] = 20
df.plot.scatter(x='ID', y='AGE')
```

65. How will you create a pie chart in pandas data frame?

We can use plot and pie() functions to create pie chart of a pandas data frame.

In following example we are creating a pie chart of a pandas data frame.

```
import numpy as np
import pandas as pd

df = pd.DataFrame()
df['ID'] = pd.Series([10,20,30], index=[1,2,3])
df['AGE'] = 20
df.plot.pie(subplots=True)
```

66. How will you read data from a CSV file in pandas?

We can use the read_csv() function to read data from a CSV (comma Separated Values) format file in pandas.

E.g. In following example we are reading iris data in pandas.

```
import pandas as pd

df=pd.read_csv('http://archive.ics.uci.edu/ml/machine-
learning-databases/iris/iris.data')
df.head(10)
```

67. What is the equivalent of SELECT LIMIT from SQL in pandas?

In SQL we use SELECT and LIMIT to select a specific number of rows from data.

In pandas, we can use head() with the number of rows to get the specific number of rows from data.

E.g. In following example we are selecting two rows from the data frame.

```
import numpy as np
import pandas as pd

df = pd.DataFrame()
df['ID'] = pd.Series([10,20,30], index=[1,2,3])
df['AGE'] = 20
df.head(2)
```

	ID	AGE
1	10	20
2	20	20

68. What is the equivalent of WHERE clause from SQL in pandas?

In SQL, we use WHERE clause to specify the filter criteria on data.

In pandas, we can use boolean indexing to filter data similar to WHERE clause in SQL.

In following example we are filtering only ID >= 20 records.

```
import numpy as np
import pandas as pd

df = pd.DataFrame()
df['ID'] = pd.Series([10,20,30], index=[1,2,3])
df['AGE'] = 20
df[df['ID'] >=20]
```

Output:

	ID	AGE
2	20	20
3	30	20

What Next?

We hope you have enjoyed the book and learnt Pandas interview questions. To complete your preparation, you might want to read our other books Data Scientist and Data Engineer interview questions.

Click this link to get the list of all of our books.

https://www.amazon.com/Knowledge-Powerhouse/e/B01N5XFZQQ/ref=dp_byline_cont_ebooks_1

Want to go higher in your career?

Take your career to the next level with these knowledgeable books on the latest technology areas.

- Top 50 Amazon AWS Interview Questions

- Microservices Interview Questions

- Top 50 Cloud Computing Interview Questions

- Top 100 Spring Interview Questions

- Top 100 GIT Interview Questions

- Top 50 Java 8 Latest Interview Questions

- Top 50 Unix Interview Questions

- Top 50 Java Design Pattern Interview Questions

- Top 100 Java Tricky Interview Questions

- Top 50 SQL Tricky Interview Questions

- Top 50 Hibernate Interview Questions

- Top 200 Java Technical Interview Questions

- Top 100 Java Collections Interview Questions

- Top 100 Java Multi-threading Interview Questions

THANKS

If you enjoyed this book in any way, then I'd like to ask you for a favor. Would you be kind enough to leave a review for this book on Amazon.com?

Link: https://www.amazon.com/Knowledge-Powerhouse/e/B01N5XFZQQ/ref=dp_byline_cont_ebooks_1

It'd be greatly appreciated!

REFERENCES

https://pandas.pydata.org/

https://www.python.org/